OFFICE FOR NATIONAL STATISTICS
SOCIAL SURVEY DIVISION

Smoking-related behaviour and attitudes

A report on research using the ONS Omnibus Survey
produced on behalf of the Department of Health

Fiona Dawe
Eileen Goddard

1997

London: The Stationery Office

Information services

For general enquiries about official statistics, please contact the Office for National Statistics Public Enquiry Service on the following telephone numbers:

Social and Economic Statistics - 0171-533 6262/6363/6364
Business Statistics   - 01633 812973

Alternatively write to Public Enquiry Service, Office for National Statistics, Zone DG/19, 1 Drummond Gate, London, SW1V 2QQ. Fax 0171-533 5719.

For more information about ONS's publications, electronic data dissemination or other information services, contact the Sales Office, Marketing and Customer Service Division, Office for National Statistics, Zone B1/06, 1 Drummond Gate, London, SW1V 2QQ. Tel 0171-533 5678 or fax 0171-533 5689.

Publications may also be obtained from The Stationery Office Publications Centre, P.O. Box 276, London, SW8 5DT. Tel 0171-873 9090 or fax 0171-873 8200.

Office for National Statistics

The Office for National Statistics (ONS) is the Government Agency responsible for compiling, analysing and disseminating many of the United Kingdom's economic, social and demographic statistics including the retail prices index, trade figures and labour market data as well as the periodic census of the population and health statistics. The head of ONS is also Registrar-General for England & Wales and the agency carries out all statutory registration of births, marriages and deaths.

ONS was formed in April 1996 from a merger of the Central Statistical Office and the Office of Population Censuses and Surveys. The Agency is independent of any other Government Department and is accountable to the Chancellor of the Exchequer.

 Government Statistical Service

ONS works in partnership with others in the Government Statistical Service (GSS) located throughout many different Government Departments. Together they provide a quality statistical service to a great many users, and this is reflected in the GSS Mission Statement:

"To provide Parliament, government and the wider community with the statistical information, analysis and advice needed to improve decision making, stimulate research and inform debate."

Each Department produces its own statistical publications, and the Office for National Statistics brings many of these statistics together in its compendia publications and databases. For further information on the source Departments, contact the ONS Public Enquiry Service on 0171-533 6262/6363.

ISBN 0 11 620948 8

Contents

Summary of key findings

Current smokers who wanted to stop *(sections 4-6)*

- 69% of current smokers said that they would like to stop smoking.

- Health was mentioned as a reason for wanting to give up by 83% of current smokers who wanted to stop smoking.

- 46% of current smokers had been given advice about giving up smoking by medical professionals - most of them by their GP.

Views about tobacco advertising *(sections 9-10)*

- 61% of respondents thought that tobacco advertising should not be allowed at all.

- Even though current smokers were more likely than other people to think that advertising of each type (on hoardings and posters, in places where cigarettes are sold, and in newspapers and magazines) should be allowed, 48% thought that tobacco advertising should not be allowed at all.

Views about tobacco sponsorship of sporting and other events *(section 11)*

- Over half of all respondents were against tobacco sponsorship - 55% disapproved of tobacco sponsorship for sports events, 61% for pop concerts and 57% for arts events, such as opera.

- Current smokers were less likely than those who had never smoked to disapprove of tobacco sponsorship - for example 43% of current smokers compared with 61% of those who had never regularly smoked thought that tobacco sponsorship of sports events should not be allowed.

Views about taxation on cigarettes *(section12)*

- 51% of respondents said that tobacco tax should be increased each year by more than the rate of inflation.

- 36% of respondents thought that tax on cigarettes should be increased by a lot more than the rate of inflation: 21% said that it should not be increased at all.

- Respondents who had never regularly smoked were much more likely than current smokers to say that tax on cigarettes should increase by more than the rate of inflation - 67% compared with 23%.

Passive smoking *(section13)*

- 84% of respondents knew that a child's risk of getting asthma was increased by passive smoking.

- 53% of respondents thought passive smoking by children increased the risk of cot death.

- 83% thought that a non-smoking adult's risk of lung cancer would be increased by passive smoking.

- Heavy smokers were less likely than other people to admit to knowing the health risks of passive smoking for children and non-smoking adults.

Restrictions on smoking *(sections 14-15)*

- At least four fifths of those interviewed agreed that there should be restrictions on smoking at work, in restaurants, and in other public places. At least two thirds of smokers were in favour of such restrictions.

- 40% of those currently working said that no smoking at all was allowed in their workplace, and a further 42% said that smoking was allowed only in designated rooms.

Smoking-related behaviour and attitudes

1 Introduction

A set of questions on various aspects of smoking behaviour and attitudes to smoking were included on the ONS Omnibus Survey in November and December 1995 and repeated in November and December 1996. This report presents the results of the 1996 survey and draws attention to any major differences compared with the 1995 findings.

2 Cigarette smoking: prevalence and consumption *(Tables 1-6)*

The key source of data for monitoring changes in the prevalence of cigarette smoking for many years has been the General Household Survey (GHS). The relevant GHS questions were included in the Omnibus as a context for interpreting the other data relating to smoking.

The prevalence of cigarette smoking as measured on the Omnibus in 1996 was 28% among both men and women - similar to both the 1995 Omnibus (28% of men and 27% of women) and the 1994 GHS (28% of men and 26% of women), although there were some differences for individual age groups. In part, these are likely to be due to a combination of the smaller size of the Omnibus, leading to higher sampling errors, and the lower response rate, which may mean that some groups, such as young men, may be less likely to be well represented. (Figure 1)

Figure 1 Prevalence of cigarette smoking, by sex and age

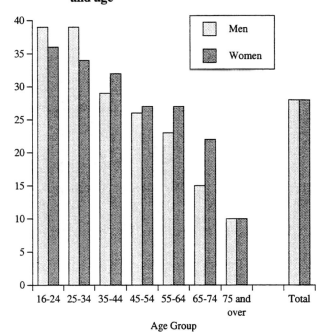

The Omnibus data on the prevalence of cigarette smoking in relation to socio-economic group showed the same strong pattern of association as does the GHS, although again there were some differences for particular groups. Most of the analysis in this report does not consider differences in, for example, attitudes, according to socio-economic group, because they are largely accounted for by the association between smoking behaviour and socio-economic group.

Almost two fifths of male smokers and just over one quarter of female smokers smoked 20 cigarettes or more a day, on average. Men were much more likely than women to smoke hand-rolled cigarettes - 21% of male smokers smoked only hand-rolled and a further 11% smoked both hand-rolled and packeted cigarettes. The equivalent figures for women were 3% and 5% respectively.

Only a handful of women smoked anything other than cigarettes, but 5% of men smoked at least one cigar a month, and 2% smoked a pipe (similar proportions to those found on the GHS). Cigar smoking was most common among men aged 35-54, and pipe smoking among men aged 65 and over.

3 Dependence *(Table 7)*

Overall, 13% of smokers said that they smoked their first cigarette within five minutes of waking up in the morning. Heavy smokers were much more likely than lighter smokers to do this: 23% of those who smoked 20 or more cigarettes a day, compared with only 2% of those who smoked fewer than 10, said that they had a cigarette within five minutes of waking.

Compared with the 1994 GHS, the 1996 Omnibus found a somewhat smaller proportion of smokers who admitted to smoking their first cigarette within five minutes of waking (13% compared with 16%).

4 Views about giving up smoking *(Tables 8-12)*

More than two thirds of current cigarette smokers said that they wanted to give up - 41% of this group saying that they wanted to do so very much. However, only 37% of those who wanted to give up thought they would be very or fairly likely to succeed if they tried in the next three months. Indeed, 25% thought they would be very unlikely to succeed.

In 1995, smokers who smoked 20 or more cigarettes a day were a little more likely than others to want to give up, but in 1996 the differences were less clearcut. However, as in 1995, those smoking 20 or more cigarettes a day were much less likely to think that they would succeed if they tried to give up: in 1996, only 7% of those who smoked 20 or more a day, compared with 32% of those who smoked fewer than 10, thought they would be very likely to succeed.

Those who wanted to give up smoking were asked why they wanted to do so. The question asked was the same as in 1995, but the pre-coded list of answers was expanded in 1996 to allow for more detailed analysis of health reasons. In 1996, 83% of smokers mentioned at least one health reason as their reason for wanting to give up: this is very similar to the proportion who mentioned health in 1995 (80%). The more detailed health codes in 1996 showed that 65% of those who wanted to give up said it was because it would be better for their health in general, 17% said that they wanted to give up because of health problems they had at present, and 29% said that the risk of getting a smoking related illness would be less if they gave up.

After health reasons the next most common reason given for wanting to give up smoking was a financial one - they could not afford it or it was a waste of money. Almost one fifth said they wanted to give up because of the effect of smoking on children.

Overall, health was equally likely to be given as a reason regardless of how much respondents smoked - suggesting that the health education message that all smoking, rather than just heavy smoking, is bad for you, is being accepted. Although women who were heavy smokers and wanted to give up were significantly more likely than other women smokers to give present health problems as a reason for wanting to do so, the base numbers are small, and this might be a chance result.

5 Attempts to stop smoking (Tables 12-13)

One half of all current cigarette smokers said they had made at least one serious attempt to stop smoking during the last five years. Just under half of those who had tried to give up had managed to do so for at least three months.

There was little difference between light and heavy smokers in the proportions who had tried to give up, but light smokers had managed to stop for longer, on average: about a fifth of those who were currently smoking fewer than ten cigarettes a day had stopped smoking for at least a year, compared with only about a tenth of those who smoked 20 or more cigarettes a day.

6 Advice from medical people (Tables 14-17)

Current smokers were asked if they had been given advice on smoking in the last five years by their GP, someone else working at the GP's surgery, a pharmacist, or any other medical person.

In 1996, 46% of all current smokers had been given advice by one or more of these people. This was an increase compared with the equivalent figure of 42% in 1995, but the difference was not statistically significant. The most common source of advice was through the general practice - in 1996, 38% had

been given advice by their own GP, and 13% by someone else at the surgery. Only 2% had been given advice on smoking by a pharmacist. In addition, 11% mentioned a variety of other medical personnel as having advised them on smoking: half of these were consultants, specialists, or other hospital doctors, and a further third were nurses.

The 1995 survey showed an association between cigarette consumption and the likelihood of having been advised about smoking, but only for women smokers. The same pattern was repeated in 1996: 59% of women who smoked 20 or more cigarettes a day had been given advice compared with 56% of those who smoked 10-19 a day, and 35% of those who smoked fewer than 10 a day. For men, there was no such pattern - the equivalent figures were 40%, 45%, and 43%. (Figure 2).

It should be noted, however, that interpretation of these data is not straightforward, in that the survey obtains current cigarette consumption, and some of those who were given advice may have cut down their smoking as a result.

Women were more likely than men to have been given advice at the surgery, but if, as is likely, advice is largely given on an opportunistic basis, this may simply reflect the fact that women are more likely than men to consult their GP (as shown by the GHS). There were no significant differences in the likelihood of having been given advice between different socio-economic groups, but those aged 45-64 were more likely to have been given advice than were younger and older smokers.

In the great majority of cases, 85%, the advice had taken the form of a discussion about smoking, rather than the respondent just being given something to take away and read. Overall, people were more likely in 1996 than in 1995 to say that they

Figure 2   Percentage who had been given advice on smoking, by sex and number of cigarettes smoked

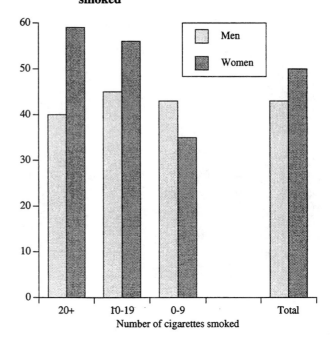

had found the advice helpful - 48% did so in 1996 compared with 37% in 1995. However, the increase occurred mainly among men - the proportion of men who had found the advice helpful rose from 36% in 1995 to 56% in 1996.

7 Ex-regular cigarette smokers *(Tables 18-21)*

One quarter of those interviewed had smoked cigarettes regularly at some time in the past. Most of them had given up a considerable time ago - indeed, 24% had stopped smoking at least 25 years ago.

These respondents were asked how many cigarettes a day they were smoking when they gave up, and 52% said they had been smoking 20 or more a day. Only 33% of current smokers said they smoked as much as this, and it is interesting to speculate about possible reasons for the difference. It is almost certainly not due to a fall over time in the consumption of those who smoke - the GHS has shown no such decline since the early 1970s. It is possible, however, that ex-smokers may overstate how much they used to smoke, to enhance their achievement in giving up. Smokers are known to under report how much they smoke, and this would tend to increase the difference even more.

The reasons given by ex-smokers for having stopped, insofar as they could remember them, were similar to the reasons given for wanting to stop by current smokers, except that they were more likely to give answers that could not be fitted into the pre-coded categories. This suggests that people's reasons for *actually* giving up smoking are more complex and varied than are reasons given by those still smoking for *wanting* to stop. (Figure 3).

There were some differences in people's reasons for giving up according to how long ago they had done so. Those who had given up more recently were more likely to give more than one reason for doing so, probably reflecting the fact that increased public awareness of the health risks of smoking has had an impact on them not only directly, but also through their families and doctors.

8 Perceptions of relative risk *(Tables 22-24)*

Respondents were asked which of a list of possible causes they thought was responsible for most premature deaths in the United Kingdom each year. The question was asked at the beginning of the section on smoking, so that respondents' answers would not be influenced by the questions on smoking behaviour and attitudes to smoking that followed. Answers to this kind of question should be interpreted with caution, however, because the concept is a difficult one which is likely to mean different things to different people.

In 1995 the question read "Which of these do you think causes the most premature deaths in the UK each year?" No definition of 'premature death' was given, and respondents probably interpreted this in varying ways according to their age and experiences. In 1996, therefore, 'premature' was defined in the question as before the age of 65 (although strictly speaking all deaths from some causes - road accidents, for example - are premature). Comparisons between 1995 and 1996 should be treated with caution because of the change in question wording and meaning.

In 1996, as in 1995, road accidents and smoking were thought to be the causes of most deaths before the age of 65: both were mentioned by 43% of respondents. The next most common answer, illicit drugs, was mentioned by only 6% of respondents. In 1995 respondents were more likely to give road accidents than smoking as the cause of most premature deaths, but the different pattern of answers in 1996 is probably due to the change in the question.

Although it is difficult to give an accurate estimate of the actual number of premature deaths attributable to each of these causes, public perceptions of deaths due to road accidents compared with those due to smoking are clearly wrong; in the UK fewer than 3,000 people under 65 die in road accidents each year, compared with estimates of 25,000 or more from smoking related causes.

Current smokers were less likely than other respondents to say that smoking was the cause of most premature deaths - 40% did so, compared with 45% of ex-smokers and 43% of those who had never smoked. These differences are less marked than those found in 1995 (and are no longer statistically significant), but this may be due to the different question wording rather than to a change in public perception of the health risks associated with smoking. The greater awareness of the health risks of smoking among ex-smokers is consistent with the finding noted earlier that most people who give up smoking do so for health reasons (see Section 4).

Figure 3 Reasons for stopping smoking, by cigarette smoking status

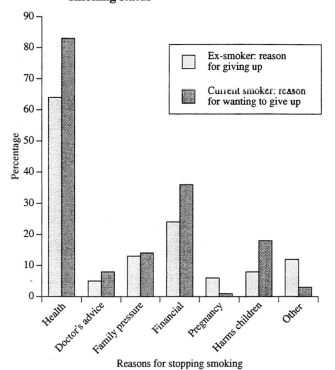

Reasons for stopping smoking

Current smokers were more likely than other respondents to say that illicit drugs were the cause of most premature deaths (8% of current smokers compared with 5% of both ex-regular smokers and those who had never smoked).

There were some interesting differences in the perceptions of men and women. Compared with men, women were less likely to say that smoking caused the most deaths under the age of 65 (39% compared with 47%) and correspondingly more likely to think that road accidents (46% compared with 41%) or illicit drugs (7% compared with 4%) did. These differences between men and women were evident in all four broad age bands - apart from road accidents where a higher proportion of men than women aged 65 and over said this was the main cause of premature deaths. It was noted above that ex-smokers were more likely than others to think smoking the main cause of premature death, and the fact that a higher proportion of men than of women are ex-smokers may explain some of the difference - though probably not among younger people.

9 Awareness of tobacco advertising restrictions *(Tables 25-27)*

An additional set of questions was introduced into the 1996 survey to measure the level of awareness of current tobacco advertising restrictions. Respondents were asked whether cigarette advertising was allowed at the following sites:

Sites where tobacco advertising is not allowed:
> television;
> cinema;
> radio;
> near schools.

Sites where tobacco advertising is allowed:
> newspapers & magazines;
> near hospitals;
> places where cigarettes are sold.

Not surprisingly, respondents were most likely to give correct answers in relation to the sites which they were likely to experience most regularly - television, radio, newspapers and magazines, and at the point of sale: more than 70% gave the correct answer in each case. In contrast, as many as 50% of respondents were unable to give an answer at all in relation to the cinema - only 34% knew that cigarette advertising was not allowed. (Figure 4).

Except for one site, more people answered correctly than incorrectly. The exception was advertising near hospitals: there is no legal restriction on such advertising, and this was included in the list to see whether people were informed about cigarette advertising restrictions or whether they were guessing, based on what they thought was likely to be the case. Only 16% said correctly that it was allowed, whereas 48% said that it was not, and 34% could not say.

Three quarters of those who said advertising was not allowed near hospitals also said that it was not allowed near schools.

Figure 4   Respondents knowledge of sites where tobacco advertising is and is not permitted

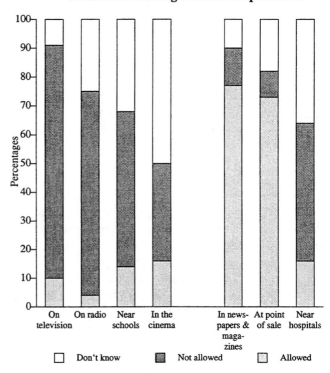

This may suggest that respondents' answers to advertising near hospitals was influenced by whether or not they thought cigarette advertising was allowed near schools - if advertising was restricted around schools it was likely that similar restrictions operated around hospitals.

Smokers were more likely to be aware of restrictions on tobacco advertisements than non-smokers. For example, 41% of current smokers knew that cigarette advertising was not allowed in the cinema compared with 34% of non-smokers. Men were slightly more likely than women to know where advertising restrictions apply (although this difference was only statistically significant for restrictions on advertising on the radio, at point of sale, and near hospitals). On the whole younger respondents were more likely than those in the older age groups to know where restrictions on advertising apply, the biggest difference between the age groups being for restrictions at the cinema - 58% of 16-24 year olds knew that advertising was not allowed compared with only 18% of those aged 65 and over. This probably reflects the fact that younger people are more likely than older people to go to the cinema.

10 Views about tobacco advertising *(Tables 28-31)*

After being asked whether they knew if cigarette advertising was allowed at various sites, respondents were asked whether they thought the government should or should not allow tobacco advertising on hoardings and posters, in places where cigarettes are sold, and in newspapers and magazines. For advertising at the point of sale, similar proportions were in favour as were against, but more than two thirds thought that the other two types of advertising should not be allowed. Indeed, 61% of respondents felt that tobacco advertising should not be allowed at all, a slight increase from 58% in 1995. However, the results show a degree of inconsistency in some respondents answers: when asked whether tobacco advertising should be allowed at point of sale only 48% felt it should not be allowed, a somewhat smaller proportion than the 61% who said that tobacco advertising should not be allowed at all. Current smokers were more likely than other respondents to think that advertising of each type should be allowed, but even so, 48% of current smokers thought that none at all should be permitted.

Respondents who knew that tobacco advertising is allowed in newspapers and magazines and at the point of sale were more likely than other respondents to think that these kinds of advertising should be permitted - probably because they were more likely to be smokers (see Section 9).

Women were considerably more likely than men to be against tobacco advertising: 65% of women compared with 55% of men. Younger people were less likely to be against tobacco advertising than older people - for example 48% of respondents aged 16-24 were against any kind of tobacco advertising compared with 70% of those aged 65 and over.

11 Views about sponsorship of sporting and other events (Tables 32-34)

Similar proportions as were against tobacco advertising disapproved of tobacco companies being given publicity in return for sponsoring sports events, pop concerts, and opera or other arts events - 55%, 61%, and 57% respectively. Only a small proportion thought that such sponsorship should be allowed - the highest figure was 17% in favour of tobacco sponsorship of sporting events. In each case, more than one

quarter of respondents gave no opinion. Just under half of all respondents (48%) thought that tobacco sponsorship of none of these events should be allowed: only 10% approved of tobacco sponsorship of all the events (this figure is not shown in any table). As with attitudes to advertising, views differed according to whether the respondent was a smoker or not: for example, only 43% of current smokers disapproved of sponsorship of sporting events, compared with 61% of those who had never smoked regularly. (Figure 5).

Again, women were more likely than men to be against tobacco sponsorship. For example 60% of women compared with 50% of men disapproved of tobacco sponsorship of sports events. Older people were more likely to disapprove of tobacco sponsorship than younger people: only 35% of respondents aged 16-24 disapproved of tobacco sponsorship of all three events compared with 55% of those aged 65 and over.

12 Views about taxation on cigarettes (Tables 35-36)

Respondents were asked how they thought tax increases on cigarettes should relate to inflation. Slightly more than one half said that tobacco tax should be increased higher than the rate of inflation. The proportion who thought that the increase should be much more than inflation was higher in 1996 than in 1995 (36% compared with 27%), but so was the proportion who said that tobacco tax should not be increased at all (21% compared with 17%).

As would be expected, there was a wide divergence of views on taxation between smokers and others: only 23% of current smokers said that taxation should be increased higher than the rate of inflation, compared with 67% of those who had never smoked. More than half those who smoked 20 a day or more said that tobacco tax should not be increased at all, but only 9% of those who had never smoked took that view. (Figure 6).

Figure 5 Percentage who disapprove of tobacco sponsorship, by smoking status

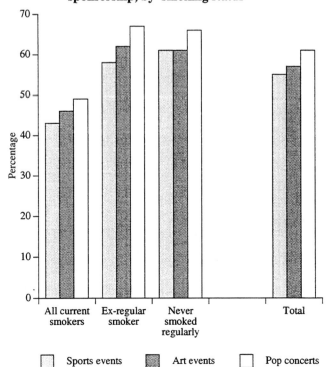

Figure 6 Respondents views on acceptable amount of tax increase, by smoking status

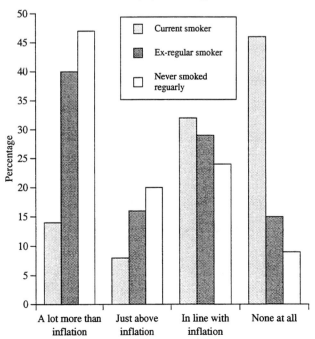

There were no marked differences according to sex. However, respondents aged 16-24 were more likely, than respondents in the other three age groups, to say that tobacco tax should not be increased at all and were less likely to say that tobacco tax should be raised a lot more than the rate of inflation.

13 Passive smoking *(Tables 37-42)*

In this section, respondents were asked whether or not they thought that living with a smoker increases a child's risk of a range of medical conditions known, or thought to be caused or exacerbated by passive smoking: asthma, glue ear, cot death, chest infections, and other infections. They were then asked a similar set of questions about the risk to adult non-smokers of the following: asthma, lung cancer, heart disease, bronchitis, and coughs and colds. One further condition was included on both lists - diabetes, the risk of which is not thought to be increased by either active or passive smoking. At both questions, about one respondent in six said they thought that the risk of becoming diabetic would increase, so the figures for other conditions should generally be taken as overstating the real level of knowledge. For some conditions, a considerable proportion of respondents were unable to say whether or not the risk would be increased by passive smoking - the highest proportion was for glue ear, when 44% could not answer. Many respondents probably did not know what this condition was - particularly those without young children.

The highest proportions of respondents - 91% and 84% respectively - thought that a child's risk of getting chest infections and asthma were increased by passive smoking. These were also the two conditions for which the proportion unable to answer was lowest - 3% and 6% respectively. (Figure 7).

For all the listed conditions, the proportion of respondents who thought that passive smoking increased risk was higher in 1996 than in 1995, although some of the changes were not statistically significant. The increase in awareness was most marked for cot death: 53% of respondents in 1996 thought that being exposed to passive smoking would increase a child's risk of cot death, compared with 46% in 1995. On the other hand, the proportion who thought passive smoking did not increase a child's risk of glue ear was slightly higher in 1996 than in 1995.

At least three-quarters of respondents thought that a non-smoking adult's risk of lung cancer, bronchitis and asthma would be increased by passive smoking. The proportion who thought that the risk of bronchitis and asthma was increased by passive smoking was higher in 1996 than in 1995 - respectively, 84% compared with 79%, and 79% compared with 76% .

Somewhat fewer - around two thirds - said that passive smoking increases the risk of heart disease and coughs and colds. Again, the proportion who thought passive smoking increases the risk of coughs and colds increased significantly between 1995 and 1996, from 63% to 68%. (Figure 8).

Heavy smokers were the least likely, and those who had never smoked the most likely, to admit to knowing the health risks of passive smoking for children and non-smoking adults. So, for example, only 63% of heavy smokers agreed that passive smoking increases a non-smoking adult's risk of getting lung cancer, compared with 91% of those who had never smoked.

Differences in awareness between men and women were small. Women were generally a little more likely to be aware of the

Figure 7 Respondents views on whether or not passive smoking increases a child's risk of certain conditions

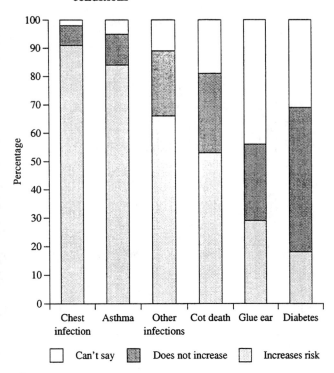

Figure 8 Respondents views on whether or not passive smoking increases a non-smoking adult's risk of certain conditions

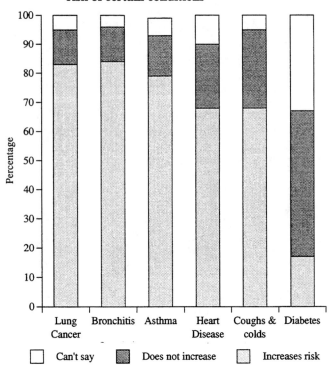

health consequences to children, and there was a marked difference for cot death: 61% of women thought the risk of cot death was increased by passive smoking, compared with only 44% of men.

On the whole, younger people were more likely to be aware of the risks of passive smoking, both to children and to adults.

14 Attitudes towards restrictions on smoking *(Tables 43-44)*

Respondents were asked whether they thought that there should be restrictions on smoking at work, in restaurants, and in other public places such as banks and post offices. For each of these locations, at least four fifths of those interviewed agreed that there should be restrictions on smoking. Even among current smokers, at least two thirds were in favour of each of these restrictions. In fact the proportion of current smokers who thought that smoking should be restricted in public places such as banks and post offices increased between 1995 and 1996 from 73% to 80%. (Figure 9).

A much smaller proportion of respondents, 48%, thought that smoking should be restricted in pubs.

Women were more likely than men to be in favour of restrictions in each of the locations, apart from in restaurants where the proportions were the same. Differences according to age were small, except that those aged 16-24 were less likely to agree with restrictions on smoking in any of the locations than were those in the older age groups. The difference between this age group and the older age groups was greatest for pubs: only 27% of respondents aged 16-24, compared with 47% of those aged 25-44, 55% of 45-64 year olds and 53% of those aged 65 and over thought smoking should be restricted in pubs.

15 Smoking in the workplace *(Tables 45-46)*

Those currently working were asked what restrictions there were on smoking where they worked: 40% said that no smoking at all was allowed on the premises, and a further 42% that it was

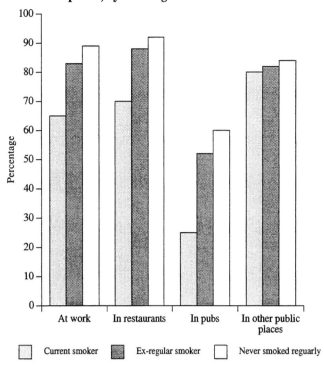

Figure 9   Percentage of respondents agreeing that smoking should be restricted in certain places, by smoking status

allowed only in designated smoking rooms. Heavy smokers were less likely than light smokers and non-smokers to work in non-smoking premises - presumably because if smoking is not possible for large parts of the working day, it is less likely that as many as 20 cigarettes in a day will be smoked.

A higher proportion of women than of men worked in a completely non-smoking environment. Respondents who were currently working and aged 65 and over were less likely, to work in buildings with designated smoking areas - this is partly due to the larger proportion of respondents in this age group, than in the other age groups, who worked on their own. However, the total number of cases in this group is very small and the results should be treated with caution. There were no significant differences between the other three age groups.

Tables

Notes to tables

1. Very small bases have been avoided wherever possible because of the relatively high sampling errors that attach to small numbers. In general, percentage distributions are shown if the base is 20 or more. Where the base is smaller than this the percentage is not given.

2. A percentage may be quoted in the text for a single category that is identifiable in the tables only by summing two or more component percentages. In order to avoid rounding errors, the percentage has been recalculated for the single category and therefore may differ by one percentage point from the sum of the percentages derived from the tables.

3. The row or column percentages may add to 99% or 101% because of rounding.

4. Unless otherwise stated, changes and differences mentioned in the text have been found to be statistically significant at the 95% confidence level.

Table 1 Cigarette smoking status, by sex: Omnibus and GHS

Cigarette smoking status	1996 Omnibus			1995 Omnibus			1994 GHS		
	Men	Women	Total	Men	Women	Total	Men	Women	Total
	%	%	%	%	%	%	%	%	%
Current cigarette smoker	28	28	28	28	27	27	28	26	27
Ex-regular cigarette smoker	32	19	26	32	19	25	31	21	26
Never or only occasionally smoked cigarettes	39	52	46	40	54	47	40	54	48
Base=100%	*1787*	*1911*	*3698*	*1879*	*2125*	*4004*	*7642*	*9108*	*16750*

Table 2 Prevalence of cigarette smoking, by sex and age: Omnibus and GHS

Age	1996 Omnibus		1995 Omnibus		1994 GHS		*Bases=100% 1996 Omnibus*		*1995 Omnibus*		*1994 GHS*	
	Men	Women	Men	Women	Men	Women	*Men*	*Women*	*Men*	*Women*	*Men*	*Women*
16-24	39	36	22	33	34	33	*218*	*218*	*242*	*248*	*996*	*1086*
25-34	39	34	39	30	34	30	*364*	*385*	*340*	*416*	*1391*	*1825*
35-44	29	32	29	28	34	28	*332*	*354*	*323*	*401*	*1470*	*1619*
45-54	26	27	34	35	26	28	*301*	*324*	*340*	*351*	*1342*	*1424*
55-64	23	27	25	22	24	24	*265*	*266*	*255*	*289*	*1035*	*1140*
65-74	15	22	21	21	19	20	*190*	*216*	*232*	*246*	*954*	*1166*
75+	10	10	14	10	14	8	*115*	*149*	*147*	*174*	*504*	*877*
Total	28	28	28	27	28	26	*1787*	*1911*	*1879*	*2125*	*7662*	*9137*

Table 3 Prevalence of cigarette smoking, by sex and socio-economic group: Omnibus and GHS

Socio-economic group	1996 Omnibus		1995 Omnibus		1994 GHS		*Bases=100% 1996 Omnibus*		*1995 Omnibus*		*1994 GHS*	
	Men	Women	Men	Women	Men	Women	*Men*	*Women*	*Men*	*Women*	*Men*	*Women*
Professional	12	19	11	12	15	13	*142*	*32*	*128*	*40*	*517*	*134*
Employers & managers	24	20	24	19	20	23	*374*	*207*	*500*	*227*	*1566*	*899*
Intermediate non-manual	23	20	27	25	24	20	*168*	*336*	*187*	*354*	*717*	*1404*
Junior non-manual	26	27	19	23	24	23	*164*	*561*	*135*	*618*	*545*	*2627*
Skilled manual	32	36	32	34	33	28	*548*	*153*	*495*	*126*	*2510*	*679*
Semi-skilled manual	39	36	36	36	37	33	*249*	*429*	*271*	*474*	*976*	*1877*
Unskilled manual	35	38	47	37	42	34	*82*	*105*	*81*	*144*	*349*	*773*
Total	28	28	28	27	28	26	*1727*	*1823*	*1797*	*1982*	*7636*	*9098*

Table 4 Daily cigarette consumption, by sex: Omnibus and GHS

Current cigarette smokers

Number of cigarettes smoked per day	1996 Omnibus		1995 Omnibus		1994 GHS	
	Men	Women	Men	Women	Men	Women
	%	%	%	%	%	%
20 or more a day	38	28	39	26	41	30
10-19 a day	37	41	40	42	36	43
Fewer than 10 a day	25	31	21	32	23	27
Base=100%	*506*	*539*	*527*	*572*	*2142*	*2332*

Table 5 Type of cigarette smoked, by sex

Current cigarette smokers

Type of cigarette	1996 Omnibus		
	Men	Women	Total
	%	%	%
Packeted	68	92	80
Hand-rolled	21	3	12
Both types	11	5	8
Base=100%	*507*	*539*	*1046*

Table 6 Prevalence of cigar and pipe smoking among men, by age

Age	Omnibus					
	Cigar smoking		Pipe smoking		*Bases=100%*	
	1996	1995	1996	1995	*1996*	*1995*
16-24	3	3	0	0	*218*	*241*
25-34	5	4	1	1	*364*	*340*
35-44	8	7	2	1	*332*	*319*
45-54	7	6	2	3	*297*	*339*
55-64	5	6	2	3	*264*	*255*
65-74	3	3	4	2	*188*	*232*
75+	5	2	7	2	*115*	*146*
Total	5	5	2	2	*1778*	*1872*
1994 GHS		6		3		*7662*

Table 7 Time between waking and the first cigarette, by sex and number of cigarettes smoked per day

Current cigarette smokers

Time between waking and the first cigarette	Number of cigarettes a day				
	20+	10-19	0-9	Total	1995 Omnibus Total
Men	%	%	%	%	%
Less than 5 minutes	23	9	2	13	13
5-14 minutes	26	13	4	16	17
15-29 minutes	24	18	5	17	17
30 mins but less than 1 hour	16	28	11	19	20
1 hour but less than 2 hours	6	20	13	13	15
2 hours or more	5	11	65	22	19
Base=100%	*192*	*187*	*126*	*505*	*525*
Women	%	%	%	%	%
Less than 5 minutes	24	12	2	12	11
5-14 minutes	27	14	4	15	14
15-29 minutes	23	16	6	15	14
30 mins but less than 1 hour	19	24	7	17	20
1 hour but less than 2 hours	5	19	17	14	14
2 hours or more	2	15	64	26	27
Base=100%	*153*	*220*	*165*	*538*	*572*
Total	%	%	%	%	%
Less than 5 minutes	23	11	2	13	12
5-14 minutes	27	14	4	15	16
15-29 minutes	23	17	5	16	15
30 mins but less than 1 hour	17	26	9	18	20
1 hour but less than 2 hours	6	20	15	14	14
2 hours or more	3	13	64	24	23
Base=100%	*345*	*406*	*292*	*1043*	*1096*

Table 8 Whether would like to give up smoking, by sex and number of cigarettes smoked per day

Current cigarette smokers

% who would like to give up	Number of cigarettes per day				
	20+	10-20	0-9	Total	1995 Omnibus Total
Men	70	76	60	70	71
Women	67	71	64	67	67
All smokers	69	73	62	69	69
Bases=100%					
Men	*190*	*187*	*126*	*503*	*520*
Women	*152*	*217*	*166*	*535*	*271*
All smokers	*342*	*405*	*292*	*1039*	*1091*

Table 9 How much would like to give up smoking, by sex and number of cigarettes smoked per day

Current cigarette smokers

How much would like to give up	Number of cigarettes per day				
	20+	10-19	0-9	Total	1995 Omnibus Total
	%	%	%	%	%
Men					
Very much indeed	37	31	22	31	27
Quite a lot	17	16	11	15	17
A fair amount	12	19	17	16	19
A little	4	11	10	8	8
Not at all	30	24	40	30	29
Base=100%	*189*	*187*	*127*	*503*	*517*
	%	%	%	%	%
Women					
Very much indeed	25	28	22	25	28
Quite a lot	25	21	17	21	18
A fair amount	11	14	18	15	13
A little	6	8	7	7	8
Not at all	33	29	36	33	33
Base=100%	*152*	*217*	*165*	*534*	*570*
	%	%	%	%	%
All smokers					
Very much indeed	31	29	22	28	26
Quite a lot	21	18	14	18	17
A fair amount	12	17	17	15	16
A little	5	9	8	8	8
Not at all	31	27	38	31	32
Base=100%	*342*	*405*	*292*	*1039*	*1087*

Table 10 Whether thinks would suceed in giving smoking up, by sex and number of cigarettes smoked per day

Smokers who want to stop

Whether thinks would succeed	Number of cigarettes per day				
	20+	10-19	0-9	Total	1995 Omnibus Total
	%	%	%	%	%
Men					
Very likely	6	14	39	16	15
Fairly likely	16	24	25	21	22
Fairly unlikely	33	30	9	26	25
Very unlikely	33	17	16	23	25
Not sure	13	15	11	13	13
Base=100%	*132*	*141*	*75*	*348*	*369*
	%	%	%	%	%
Women					
Very likely	8	7	27	13	15
Fairly likely	16	18	34	22	20
Fairly unlikely	26	32	25	29	23
Very unlikely	39	33	10	28	25
Not sure	12	10	3	8	16
Base=100%	*103*	*152*	*106*	*361*	*379*
	%	%	%	%	%
All smokers					
Very likely	7	10	32	15	15
Fairly likely	16	21	30	22	21
Fairly unlikely	30	31	19	27	24
Very unlikely	35	25	13	25	25
Not sure	12	12	6	11	15
Base=100%	*234*	*296*	*181*	*711*	*748*

Table 11 Main reasons for wanting to stop smoking, by sex and number of cigarettes smoked per day

Smokers who want to stop

Reasons for wanting to stop	Number of cigarettes per day			Total	1995 Omnibus Total*
	20+	10-19	0-9		
	%	%	%	%	%
Men					
Present health problems	19	13	21	17	
Better for health in general	62	70	55	64	
Less risk of getting smoking related illness	33	31	31	32	
At least one health reason	**86**	**83**	**81**	**83**	**80†**
Doctor's advice	8	5	10	7	9
Family pressure	7	15	27	15	18
Financial reasons	44	36	15	34	37
Pregnancy	1	1	0	1	0
Harms children	17	14	10	14	20
Other	3	5	5	4	4
Gave more than one reason	**62**	**62**	**47**	**59**	
Base=100%	*133*	*143*	*75*	*351*	*367*
	%	%	%	%	%
Women					
Present health problems	22	15	12	16	
Better for health in general	59	69	67	65	
Less risk of getting smoking related illness	26	24	29	26	
At least one health reason	**84**	**81**	**83**	**83**	**81†**
Doctor's advice	12	7	7	9	10
Family pressure	9	11	22	14	16
Financial reasons	46	40	26	37	40
Pregnancy	0	3	1	2	2
Harms children	25	22	18	22	21
Other	0	1	4	2	4
Gave more than one reason	**59**	**62**	**58**	**60**	
Base=100%	*102*	*153*	*106*	*361*	*380*
	%	%	%	%	%
All smokers					
Present health problems	20	14	16	17	
Better for health in general	61	69	62	65	
Less risk of getting smoking related illness	30	27	30	29	
At least one health reason	**85**	**82**	**82**	**83**	**80†**
Doctor's advice	10	6	8	8	9
Family pressure	8	13	24	14	17
Financial reasons	45	38	21	36	38
Pregnancy	0	2	1	1	2
Harms children	20	18	14	18	21
Other	2	3	5	3	4
Gave more than one reason	**60**	**62**	**52**	**59**	
Base=100%	*235*	*296*	*181*	*712*	*747*

Percentages sum to more than 100 as respondents could give more than one answer.
* The health categories were expanded in 1996.
† The 1995 figure is for those who said 'Health reasons'.

Table 12 Percentage who had tried to give up smoking in the last 5 years, by sex and number of cigarettes smoked per day

Current cigarette smokers

% who had tried to give up	Number of cigarettes per day				
	20+	10-19	0-9	Total	1995 Omnibus Total
Men	47	51	47	48	48
Women	50	58	50	53	53
All smokers	48	55	49	51	51
Bases=100%					
Men	*192*	*187*	*126*	*505*	*527*
Women	*153*	*220*	*166*	*539*	*572*
All smokers	*345*	*406*	*292*	*1043*	*1091*

Table 13 Longest time stopped smoking in the last 5 years, by number of cigarettes smoked per day

Cigarette smokers who had tried to stop

Longest time stopped	Number of cigarettes per day				
	20+	10-19	0-9	Total	1995 Omnibus Total
	%	%	%	%	%
Less than a week	24	13	11	16	16
1-3 weeks	28	21	15	22	20
About a month	4	8	6	6	8
1-2 months	12	13	14	13	9
3-5 months	10	18	19	16	17
6-11 months	14	13	15	14	14
A year or more	9	14	21	14	17
Base=100%	*167*	*222*	*140*	*529*	*547*

Table 14 Percentage who had been given advice on smoking in the last 5 years, by sex

Current smokers

Source of advice	Men	Women	Total	1995 Omnibus Total
	1996	1996	1996	
	%	%	%	%
GP	34	42	38	35
Someone else at the surgery	11	15	13	10
Pharmacist	2	2	2	2
Other medical person	11	10	11	9
Any of the above	43	50	46	42
Base=100%	*507*	*540*	*1047*	*1099*

Percentages sum to more than the 'Any of the above' total as respondents could give more than one answer

16

Table 15 Percentage who had been given advice on smoking, by sex and number of cigarettes smoked per day

Current smokers

| | Number of cigarettes per day | | | | |
	20+	10-19	0-9	Total	1995 Omnibus Total
% given advice by GP					
Men	33	35	34	34	32
Women	55	45	27	42	37
All smokers	43	41	30	38	35
% given any advice by any medical person					
Men	40	45	43	43	38
Women	59	56	35	50	45
All smokers	48	51	38	46	42
Base=100%					
Men	*192*	*187*	*127*	*506*	*527*
Women	*153*	*220*	*167*	*540*	*572*
All smokers	*345*	*407*	*292*	*1044*	*1099*

Table 16 Percentage who had been given advice on smoking in the last 5 years, by a) age, b) socio-economic group

Current smokers

| | % who had been given advice | | Base=100% | |
	1995	1996	1995	1996
a) Age				
16-44	44	44	*599*	*644*
45-64	40	52	*364*	*299*
65 and over	39	43	*137*	*103*
b) Socio-economic group				
Professional	..	57	*19*	*23*
Employers & managers	42	51	*162*	*130*
Intermediate non-manual	49	48	*140*	*106*
Junior non-manual	40	46	*168*	*196*
Skilled manual	43	42	*203*	*229*
Semi-skilled manual	41	44	*269*	*254*
Unskilled manual	43	57	*92*	*69*
Total	42	47	*1099*	*1007*

Table 17 Type of advice given, and whether it was helpful or not, by sex

Those given advice

| Nature of advice | Men | | Women | | Total | |
	1995	1996	1995	1996	1995	1996
	%	%	%	%	%	%
Type of advice						
Discussion	79	86	81	83	80	85
Literature only	21	14	19	17	20	15
	%	%	%	%	%	%
Whether helpful						
Yes	36	56	38	42	37	48
No	64	44	62	58	63	52
Base=100%	*267*	*252*	*315*	*303*	*582*	*555*

Table 18 Length of time since stopped smoking, by sex

Ex-regular cigarette smokers

Length of time since stopped	Men	Women	Total	1995 Omnibus Total
	%	%	%	%
Less than a year	6	7	6	7
1-4 years	12	19	15	15
5-9 years	13	14	13	16
10-14 years	15	13	14	16
15-19 years	12	11	12	12
20-24 years	16	15	15	10
25 years or more	26	22	24	23
Base=100%	*580*	*370*	*950*	*993*

Table 19 Number of cigarettes smoked a day when a smoker, by sex

Ex-regular cigarette smokers

Number of cigarettes smoked	Men	Women	Total	1995 Omnibus Total
	%	%	%	%
20 or more a day	61	37	52	50
10-19 a day	27	38	32	33
Fewer than 10 a day	12	25	17	16
Base=100%	*571*	*368*	*939*	*1009*

Table 20 Main reasons for having stopped smoking, by sex

Ex-regular cigarette smokers

Reasons for having stopped	Men	Women	Total	1995 Omnibus Total*
	%	%	%	%
Present health problems	15	14	15	
Better for health in general	52	44	48	
Less risk of getting smoking related illness	12	11	12	
At least one health reason	**67**	**60**	**64**	**63†**
Doctor's advice	6	3	5	8
Family pressure	13	14	13	12
Financial reasons	23	24	24	20
Pregnancy	1	14	6	7
Harms Children	7	9	8	6
Other	12	11	12	17
Gave more than one reason	**30**	**34**	**32**	
Base=100%	*576*	*368*	*944*	*1038*

Percentages sum to more than 100 as respondents could give more than one answer.
* The health categories were expanded in 1996.
† The 1995 figure is for those who said "Health reasons".

Table 21 Main reasons for having stopped smoking, by length of time since stopped

Ex-regular cigarette smokers

Reasons for having stopped	Length of time since stopped			
	Less than 5 years	5-19 years	20 years or more	Total
	%	%	%	%
Present health problems	23	17	8	15
Better for health in general	50	47	48	48
Less risk of getting smoking related illness	15	11	12	12
At least one health reason	**74**	**65**	**57**	**64**
Doctor's advice	4	7	2	5
Family pressure	16	17	9	13
Financial reasons	23	21	26	24
Pregnancy	8	6	5	6
Harms children	11	6	7	8
Other	6	12	16	12
Gave more than one reason	**40**	**33**	**27**	**32**
Base=100%	*204*	*366*	*375*	*944*

Percentages sum to more than 100 as respondents could give more than one answer.

Table 22 What respondents think is the main cause of deaths before the age of 65 in the UK, by smoking status

Main cause of premature death before age 65	Smoking status						
	Heavy smoker	Light smoker	All current smokers	Ex-regular Smoker	Never smoked regularly	Total	1995 Omnibus Total*
	%	%	%	%	%	%	%
Road accidents	39	44	43	41	44	43	44
Accidents at work	2	2	2	3	2	2	2
AIDS	1	1	1	1	1	1	2
Smoking	43	39	40	45	43	43	37
Murder/manslaughter	2	1	2	1	1	1	3
Illicit drugs	9	8	8	5	5	6	8
Alcohol misuse	4	4	4	3	4	4	4
Base=100%	*340*	*687*	*1028*	*926*	*1670*	*3624*	*3956*

* The question in 1995 did not define 'premature death', in 1996 the question defined premature deaths as those occuring before the age of 65.

Table 23 What respondents think is the main cause of deaths before the age of 65 in the UK, by sex and age

Main cause of death before age 65	Men					Women				
	16-24	25-44	45-64	65+	Total	16-24	25-44	45-64	65+	Total
	%	%	%	%	%	%	%	%	%	%
Road accidents	38	42	37	46	41	54	48	40	43	46
Accidents at work	2	2	1	6	2	2	2	2	3	2
AIDS	2	1	1	2	1	0	1	1	2	1
Smoking	45	47	51	36	47	32	40	47	30	39
Murder/manslaughter	2	1	1	1	1	1	1	1	3	1
Illicit drugs	5	4	4	7	4	8	5	6	13	7
Alcohol misuse	6	4	4	2	4	2	3	3	5	3
Base=100%	216	685	556	295	1752	215	731	575	348	1869

Table 24 What respondents think is the main cause of deaths before the age of 65 in the UK, by age

Main cause of death before age 65	Age							
	16-24	25-34	35-44	45-54	55-64	65-74	75+	Total
	%	%	%	%	%	%	%	%
Road accidents	46	45	45	37	41	44	45	43
Accidents at work	2	2	2	1	1	4	6	2
AIDS	1	1	1	1	2	3	1	1
Smoking	39	43	45	52	46	35	29	43
Murder/manslaughter	1	1	1	0	2	2	3	1
Illicit drugs	7	4	4	5	6	10	12	6
Alcohol misuse	4	4	2	4	3	3	4	4
Base=100%	430	742	674	609	522	398	246	3621

Table 25 Knowledge of sites where tobacco advertising is and is not permitted

Site	Respondents' opinions as to whether advertising is allowed			
	Allowed	Not Allowed	Don't know	*Base (=100%)*
Sites where advertising is not allowed				
.... on television %	10	**81**	9	*3698*
.... on radio %	4	**71**	25	*3698*
.... near schools %	14	**54**	32	*3698*
.... in the cinema %	16	**34**	50	*3698*
Sites where advertising is allowed				
.... in newspapers & magazines %	**76**	13	10	*3698*
.... at point of sale %	**73**	9	18	*3698*
.... near hospitals %	**16**	48	36	*3698*

Table 26 Percentage of respondents who knew whether cigarette advertising was allowed, by site and smoking status

Site	Smoking status					
	Heavy smoker	Light smoker	All current smokers	Ex-regular smokers	Never smoked regularly	Total
	%	%	%	%	%	%
% who knew advertising is not allowed						
.... on television	86	82	83	83	80	81
.... on radio	77	75	76	68	70	71
.... near schools	57	57	57	51	54	54
.... in the cinema	41	40	41	27	34	34
% who knew advertising is allowed						
.... in newspapers & magazines	79	81	81	72	76	76
.... at point of sale	80	77	78	75	69	73
.... near hospitals	13	15	14	17	16	16
Base=100%	345	699	1047	946	1705	3696

Table 27 Percentage of respondents who knew whether cigarette advertising was allowed, by site and by sex and age

Site	Sex		Age				
	Male	Female	16-24	25-44	45-64	65 +	Total
% who knew advertising is not allowed							
.... on television	82	81	76	86	83	71	81
.... on radio	74	68	76	79	69	54	71
.... near schools	54	53	62	56	52	46	54
.... in the cinema	35	33	58	42	25	18	34
% who knew advertising is allowed							
.... in newspapers & magazines	77	76	86	83	73	61	76
.... at point of sale	77	70	83	77	71	62	73
.... near hospitals	18	14	13	17	16	14	16
Base=100%	*1786*	*1911*	*437*	*1433*	*1157*	*670*	*3697*

Table 28 Respondents views on whether tobacco advertising should be allowed

Site		Should be allowed	Should not be allowed	Don't know	Base (=100%)
Hoardings & posters	%	29	68	3	*3697*
At point of sale	%	49	48	3	*3698*
Newspapers & magazines	%	30	67	2	*3697*
Any kind of advertising	%	37	61	2	*3697*

Table 29 Percentage of respondents who said the government should not allow tobacco advertising, by site and smoking status

Site	Smoking status						
	Heavy smoker	Light smoker	All current smokers	Ex-regular smoker	Never smoked regularly	Total	1995 Omnibus Total
Hoardings & posters	56	59	58	73	72	68	69
At point of sale	39	37	37	50	53	48	52
Newspapers & magazines	59	58	58	71	71	67	68
Any kind of advertising	51	47	48	66	65	61	58
Base=100%	*345*	*699*	*1046*	*946*	*1705*	*3697*	*3956*

Table 30 Percentage of respondents who said the government should not allow tobacco advertising, by site and by sex and age

Site	Sex		Age				
	Male	Female	16-24	25-44	45-64	65 & over	Total
Hoardings & posters	65	71	60	67	69	74	68
At point of sale	43	52	31	46	51	57	48
Newspapers & magazines	64	70	60	64	69	74	67
Any kind of advertising	55	65	48	58	63	70	61
Base=100%	*1786*	*1912*	*437*	*1433*	*1157*	*670*	*3697*

Table 31 Respondents who knew that tobacco advertising is allowed in newspapers and magazines, and at the point of sale: whether they thought such advertising should or should not be allowed

Respondents who knew tobacco advertising was allowed

Views on whether government should allow tobacco advertising	Respondents who knew tobacco advertising was allowed	
	Newspapers & magazines	Place of Sale
	%	%
Should allow	34	55
Shouldn't allow	64	42
Don't know	2	2
Base=100%	*2825*	*2702*

Table 32 Respondents views on whether tobacco sponsorship should be allowed

Type of event		Should be allowed	Should not be allowed	Don't know	Base (=100%)
Sports events	%	17	55	28	*3698*
Pop concerts	%	12	61	26	*3696*
Arts events	%	14	57	29	*3696*

Table 33 Percentage of respondents who disapprove of tobacco sponsorship, by smoking status

Type of sponsorship	Smoking status						
	Heavy smoker	Light smoker	All current smokers	Ex-regular smoker	Never smoked regularly	Total	1995 Omnibus Total
	%	%	%	%	%	%	%
Sports events	40	45	43	58	61	55	54
Pop concerts	47	50	49	67	66	61	62
Arts events	45	46	46	62	61	57	57
Proportion who dissapproved of tobacco sponsorship for all 3 events	34	37	36	52	54	48	
Base=100%	345	700	1047	946	1705	3969	3956

Table 34 Percentage of respondents who disapprove of tobacco sponsorship, by sex and age

Type of event	Sex		Age				
	Men	Women	16-24	25-44	45-64	65+	Total
	Percentage who disapproved of tobacco sponsorships						
Sports events	50	60	51	53	57	60	55
Pop concerts	58	65	49	59	65	68	61
Arts events	52	61	44	53	61	66	57
Percentage who dissaproved of tobacco sponsorship for all 3 events	43	53	35	46	53	55	48
Base=100%	1786	1912	437	1433	1157	670	3697

Table 35 Views on acceptable amount of tax increase, by smoking status

Amount of tax increase that is acceptable	Smoking status						
	Heavy smoker	Light smoker	All current smokers	Ex-regular smoker	Never smoked regularly	Total	1995 Omnibus Total
	%	%	%	%	%	%	%
A lot more than inflation	13	15	14	40	47	36	27
Just above inflation	5	10	8	16	20	16	22
In line with inflation	26	35	32	29	24	28	34
None at all	57	40	46	15	9	21	17
Base=100%	341	691	1034	921	1656	3611	3956

Table 36 Views on acceptable amount of tax increase, by sex and age

Amount of increase that is acceptable	Sex		Age				
	Men	Women	16-24	25-44	45-64	65+	Total
	%	%	%	%	%	%	%
A lot more than inflation	36	36	23	36	39	38	36
Just above inflation	16	15	19	16	15	13	16
In line with inflation	27	28	26	29	26	29	28
None at all	21	21	32	19	20	19	21
Base=100%	1754	1857	426	1414	1129	642	3612

21

Table 37 Views on whether or not passive smoking increases a child's risk of certain medical conditions

Condition		Increases risk	Does not increase risk	Can't say	Base=100%
1996 Omnibus					
Chest infection	%	91	7	3	3696
Asthma	%	84	11	6	3696
Other infections	%	66	23	12	3696
Cot death	%	53	28	19	3696
Glue ear	%	29	27	44	3696
Diabetes	%	18	51	32	3696
1995 Omnibus					
Chest infection	%	88	8	4	4010
Asthma	%	81	13	7	4010
Other infections	%	63	24	12	4010
Cot death	%	46	32	22	4010
Glue ear	%	28	24	48	4010
Diabetes	%	16	49	34	4010

Table 38 Views on whether or not passive smoking increases a child's risk of certain conditions, by smoking status

Whether increases risk	Omnibus 1996					
	Smoking status					
	Heavy smoker	Light smoker	All current smokers	Ex-regular smoker	Never smoked regularly	Total
Yes						
Chest infections	81	85	83	94	93	91
Asthma	66	75	72	86	90	84
Other infections	54	57	56	69	70	66
Cot death	39	47	44	47	61	53
Glue ear	21	24	23	32	32	29
Diabetes	11	14	13	18	20	18
No						
Chest infection	16	12	13	5	4	7
Asthma	26	18	21	10	5	11
Other infections	36	29	31	20	19	23
Cot death	43	36	38	30	20	28
Glue ear	41	32	35	25	23	27
Diabetes	65	60	62	47	46	51
Can't say						
Chest infections	3	4	3	2	3	3
Asthma	8	7	7	5	5	5
Other infections	10	14	13	12	11	12
Cot death	18	17	17	22	19	19
Glue ear	38	44	42	44	45	44
Diabetes	24	26	25	36	33	32
Base=100%	*345*	*699*	*1046*	*947*	*1704*	*3697*

Table 39 Views on whether or not passive smoking increases a child's risk of certain medical conditions, by sex and age

Whether increases risk	Sex		Age				
	Men	Women	16-24	25-44	45-64	65+	Total
Yes							
Chest infections	91	90	91	92	90	88	91
Asthma	83	84	85	85	82	81	84
Other infections	68	64	65	68	64	64	66
Cot death	44	61	50	59	51	45	53
Glue ear	28	31	25	29	30	31	29
Diabetes	19	16	13	15	18	26	18
No							
Chest infections	7	7	6	7	7	7	7
Asthma	11	10	10	10	12	11	11
Other infections	21	24	24	22	24	21	23
Cot death	34	22	29	26	28	30	28
Glue ear	25	28	24	30	25	24	27
Diabetes	49	52	61	56	47	38	51
Can't say							
Chest infections	2	3	3	2	2	5	3
Asthma	6	5	5	4	6	8	6
Other infections	11	12	11	10	12	14	12
Cot death	22	17	20	15	21	25	19
Glue ear	47	41	51	40	45	45	44
Diabetes	31	32	27	29	34	37	32
Base=100%	*1791*	*1915*	*439*	*1160*	*1160*	*673*	*3706*

Table 40 Views on whether or not passive smoking increases a non-smoking adult's risk of certain conditions

Condition		Increases risk	Does not increase risk	Can't say	*Base=100%*
1996 Omnibus					
Lung cancer	%	83	12	5	*3696*
Bronchitis	%	84	12	4	*3696*
Asthma	%	79	14	6	*3696*
Heart disease	%	68	22	10	*3696*
Coughs & colds	%	68	27	5	*3696*
Diabetes	%	17	50	33	*3696*
1995 Omnibus					
Lung cancer	%	82	13	5	*4010*
Bronchitis	%	79	11	10	*4010*
Asthma	%	76	17	7	*4010*
Heart disease	%	67	22	10	*4010*
Coughs & colds	%	63	27	10	*4010*
Diabetes	%	17	49	34	*4010*

Table 41 Views on whether or not passive smoking increases a non-smoking adult's risk of certain conditions, by smoking status

Whether increases risk	Smoking status					
	Heavy smoker	Light smoker	All current smokers	Ex-regular smoker	Never smoked regularly	Total
Yes						
Lung cancer	63	75	71	82	91	83
Bronchitis	71	75	73	86	90	84
Asthma	62	68	66	81	87	79
Heart disease	53	59	57	72	73	68
Coughs & colds	53	62	59	70	73	68
Diabetes	11	15	14	16	21	17
No						
Lung cancer	31	19	23	13	5	12
Bronchitis	25	18	20	10	7	12
Asthma	31	23	25	13	8	14
Heart disease	38	30	33	20	17	22
Coughs & colds	42	34	37	25	21	27
Diabetes	69	57	61	47	44	50
Can't say						
Lung cancer	6	7	6	5	4	5
Bronchitis	5	6	6	3	4	4
Asthma	8	9	9	6	5	6
Heart disease	9	11	10	8	10	10
Coughs & colds	4	4	4	5	6	5
Diabetes	20	28	25	37	35	33
Base=100%	*344*	*700*	*1046*	*946*	*1705*	*3697*

Table 42 Views on whether or not passive smoking increases a non-smoking adult's risk of certain conditions, by sex and age

Whether increases risk	Sex		Age				
	Men	Women	16-24	25-44	45-64	65+	Total
Yes							
Lung cancer	84	82	92	85	81	77	83
Bronchitis	84	85	83	85	85	82	84
Asthma	80	79	83	80	78	77	79
Heart disease	71	65	68	69	68	66	68
Coughs & colds	68	68	70	70	66	68	68
Diabetes	19	16	17	14	18	24	17
No							
Lung cancer	12	12	5	11	14	15	12
Bronchitis	12	11	10	11	12	13	12
Asthma	14	14	11	15	16	14	14
Heart disease	20	25	21	23	23	21	22
Coughs & colds	27	27	24	26	29	24	27
Diabetes	49	50	53	55	48	40	50
Can't say							
Lung cancer	4	6	3	4	5	7	5
Bronchitis	4	4	7	3	3	5	4
Asthma	6	6	6	5	6	9	6
Heart disease	9	10	11	8	9	12	10
Coughs & colds	5	5	6	4	4	8	5
Diabetes	32	34	30	31	34	36	33
Base=100%	*1785*	*1911*	*436*	*1433*	*1237*	*799*	*3096*

Table 43 Percentage agreeing that smoking should be restricted in certain places, by smoking status

Smoking should be restricted (% agreeing)	Smoking status					
	Heavy smoker	Light smoker	All current smokers	Ex-regular smoker	Never smoked regularly	Total
1996 Omnibus						
... at work	55	70	65	83	89	81
... in restaurants	64	73	70	88	92	85
... in pubs	19	28	25	52	60	48
... in other public places	74	83	80	82	84	82
Base=100%	*344*	*700*	*1046*	*946*	*1704*	*3696*
1995 Omnibus						
... at work	58	68	65	85	92	83
... in restaurants	62	73	70	90	94	86
... in pubs	24	25	25	54	63	50
... in other public places	64	76	73	81	86	81
Base=100%	*354*	*738*	*1092*	*1003*	*1885*	*3980*

Table 44 Percentages agreeing that smoking should be restricted in certain places, by sex and by age

Smoking should be restricted (% agreeing)	Sex		Age				
	Men	Women	16-24	25-44	45-64	65+	Total
... at work	79	82	71	82	83	79	81
... in restaurants	85	85	77	84	87	89	85
... in pubs	47	50	27	47	55	53	48
... in other public places	80	84	78	84	83	82	82
Base=100%	*1784*	*1912*	*437*	*1434*	*1156*	*671*	*3696*

24

Table 45 Restrictions on smoking where respondent currently works, by smoking status

Those currently working

Whether increases risk	Smoking status					Total	1995 Omnibus Total
	Heavy smoker	Light smoker	All current smokers	Ex-regular smoker	Never smoked regularly		
No smoking at all	20	33	29	43	45	40	38
Designated areas only	51	51	51	35	40	42	43
No restrictions at all	23	13	16	15	11	13	15
Don't know with others	6	4	5	7	5	5	5
Base=100%	191	423	614	497	1043	2154	2224

Table 46 Restrictions on smoking where respondent currently works, by sex and age

Those currently working

Level of restriction	Sex		Age				Total
	Men	Women	16-24	25-44	45-64	65+	
	%	%	%	%	%	%	%
No smoking at all	33	47	41	38	42	45	40
Designated areas only	42	41	45	45	37	11	42
No restrictions at all	18	7	11	12	15	21	13
Don't work with others	6	4	3	5	5	23	5
Base = 100%	1164	990	288	1089	729	47	2154

25

Annex A   The ONS Omnibus Survey

The Omnibus Survey is a multi-purpose survey carried out by the Office for National Statistics for use by Government departments and other public or non-profit making bodies. Interviewing is carried out every month and each month's questionnaire covers a variety of topics, reflecting different user's requirements.

The sample

A random probability sample of 3,000 private households in Great Britain is selected each month using the Postcode Address File as a sampling frame. One hundred new postal sectors are selected and are stratified by region, the proportion of households renting from the local authorities and the proportion in which the head of household is in Socio-Economic Groups 1-5 or 13 (that is a professional employer or manager). The postal sectors are selected with probability proportional to size and within each sector 30 addresses are selected randomly.

Within households with more than one adult member, one person aged 16 or over is randomly selected for interview. No proxy interviews are taken.

Weighting

Because only one household member is interviewed at each address, people in households containing few adults have a higher probability of selection than those in households with many. Where the unit of analysis is individual adults, as it is for this module, a weighting factor is applied to correct for this unequal probability of selection.

Fieldwork

Interviews are carried out face-to-face by interviewers trained to carry out a range of ONS surveys. The Omnibus Survey uses computer assisted interviewing which has well documented effects on the quality of the data.

Questions

The module of questions (which are shown in Annex B) was developed in conjunction with the Department of Health.

Response Rates

The small users' Postal Address File includes some business addresses and other address, such as new and empty properties, at which no private households are living. The expected proportion of such addresses, which are classified as ineligible. is about 11-12%. This figure is removed before the response rate is calculated.

The response rate for the November and December 1996 Omnibus surveys was 70%, as shown below:

Set sample	**6,000**	**100%**
Ineligible addresses	681	11%
Eligible addresses	**5,319**	**100%**
Refusals	1,203	23%
Non-contacts	410	8%
Respondents	**3,706**	**70%**

Annex B: The Questions

ask always:

m130–1   THIS MODULE IS FOR THE DEPARTMENT
OF HEALTH
Which of these do you think causes the most
deaths before the age of 65 in the UK each year?

(1) Road accidents
(2) Accidents at work
(3) AIDS
(4) Smoking
(5) Murder and manslaughter
(6) Illicit drugs
(7) Alcohol misuse

ask always:

M130–2   Do you smoke cigarettes at all nowadays?

(1) Yes
(2) No

ask if: smoker nowadays

m130–3   How many cigarettes a day do you usually smoke
at weekends?

0..200

ask if: smoker nowadays

m130–4   How many cigarettes a day do you usually smoke
on weekdays?

0..200

ask if: smoker nowadays

m130–5   Do you usually smoke packeted cigarettes, hand-
rolled cigarettes or both types?

(1) Packeted
(2) Hand-rolled
(3) Both types

ask if: not smoker nowadays

m130–6   Have you ever smoked cigarettes regularly?

(1) Yes
(2) No

ask if: not smoker nowadays and ever smoked regularly

m130–7   About how many cigarettes a day did you smoke
when you smoked regularly?

0..200

ask always:

m130–8   Do you smoke at least one cigar of any kind per
month nowadays?

(1) Yes
(2) No

ask men only

m130–9   Do you smoke a pipe at all nowadays?

(1) Yes
(2) No

ask if: smokes cigarettes nowadays

m130–10   How soon after waking do you smoke your first
cigarette of the day?

(1) Less than 5 minutes
(2) 5-14 minutes
(3) 15-29 minutes
(4) 30 mins but less than 1 hour
(5) 1 hour but less than 2 hours
(6) 2 hours or more

ask if: smokes nowadays - cigarrettes, cigars, or pipe

m130–11   Would you like to give up smoking?

(1) Yes
(2) No

*ask if: smokes nowadays - cigarrettes, cigars, or pipe and like to
give up*

m130–12   How much would you like to give up smoking, ...
a little, a fair amount, quite a lot, or very much
indeed?

RUNNING PROMPT

(1) a little
(2) a fair amount
(3) quite a lot
(4) very much indeed

ask if: smokes nowadays - cigarrettes, cigars, or pipe and like to give up

m130–13   What are your main reasons for wanting to give up?

CODE UP TO 3 OF
(1)   because of a health problem I have at present
(2)   better for my health in general
(3)   less risk of getting smoking related illnesses
(4)   doctor said I should stop
(5)   family/friends wanted me to stop
(6)   financial reasons (couldn't afford it)
(7)   pregnancy
(8)   worried about the effect on my children
(9)   other (specify)

ask if: smokes nowadays - cigarrettes, cigars, or pipe and like to give up and 'Other' at m130–13

spec13   Please specify other reasons

ask if: smokes nowadays - cigarrettes, cigars, or pipe and like to give up

m130–14   If you tried to give up in, say, the next three months, how likely do you think you would be to succeed?

(1)   Very likely
(2)   Fairly likely
(3)   Fairly unlikely
(4)   Very unlikely
(5)   Not sure

ask if: smokes nowadays - cigarrettes, cigars, or pipe

m130–15   Have you made a serious attempt to give up smoking in the last five years, that is since November/December 1991?

(1)   Yes
(2)   No

ask if: smokes nowadays - cigarrettes, cigars, or pipe and made attempt to give up

M130–16   How many times have you tried to stop (in the last 5 years)?

0..10

ask if: smokes nowadays - cigarrettes, cigars, or pipe and Made attempt to give up

M130–17   What is the longest period you've managed to give up for (in the last five years)?

(1)   A few days - less than a week
(2)   About a week
(3)   About two or three weeks
(4)   About a month
(5)   More than a month

ask if: smokes nowadays - cigarrettes, cigars, or pipe and made attempt to give up and 'more than a month' at M130–17

SPEC17   Please specify the number of months or years

ask if: has given up smoking

m130–18   How long ago is it since you stopped smoking cigarettes?
PLEASE RECORD WHETHER YEARS MONTHS OR WEEKS AGO AND ACTUALLY HOW LONG AT NEXT QUESTION IF LESS THAN A WEEK RECORD AS ZERO WEEKS

(1)   years
(2)   months
(3)   weeks

ask if: has given up smoking

INT18   How many years/months/weeks ago was this
ASK OR CODE THE NUMBER HERE

1..99

ask if: has given up smoking

m130–19   Was that your first serious attempt at stopping, or had you tried to give up smoking cigarettes before then?

(1)   First attempt
(2)   Tried before

ask if: has given up smoking

m130–20   On the whole, did you find it easy or difficult to give up smoking cigarettes? Was it ..
RUNNING PROMPT

(1)   Very easy
(2)   Fairly easy
(3)   Fairly difficult
(4)   Very difficult
(5)   Not sure/can't remember

ask if: has given up smoking

m130–21   What were your main reasons for wanting to give up smoking cigarettes?

CODE UP TO 3 OF
(1)   because of a health problem I have at present
(2)   better for my health in general
(3)   less risk of getting smoking related illnesses
(4)   doctor said I should stop
(5)   family/friends wanted me to stop
(6)   financial reasons (couldn't afford it)
(7)   pregnancy
(8)   worried about the effect on my children
(9)   other (specify)

ask if: has given up smoking and 'Other' at M130–21

spec21   Please specify other reasons

ask if: smokes now or if gave up less than 5 years ago

m130–22a   In the last 5 years, have you been given advice on smoking by your GP?

    (1) Yes
    (2) No

ask if: smokes now or if gave up less than 5 years ago

m130–22b   (In the last 5 years, have you been given advice on smoking by) someone else who works at the surgery or health centre?

    (1) Yes
    (2) No

ask if: smokes now or if gave up less than 5 years ago

m130–22c   (In the last 5 years, have you been given advice on smoking by) a pharmacist?

    (1) Yes
    (2) No

ask if: smokes now or if gave up less than 5 years ago

m130–22d   (In the last 5 years, have you been given advice on smoking by) any other medical person?

    (1) Yes
    (2) No

ask if: smokes now or if gave up less than 5 years ago and 'Yes' at m130–22d

SPEC22d   Please specify who the other medical person was

ask if: smokes now or if gave up less than 5 years ago and any advice given by GP or any other relevant person

M130–23   And may I just check,was the advice you received part of general health advice or was it connected with a particular health problem you were concerned about?

    (1) General advice
    (2) Particular health problem
    (3) Both

ask if: smokes now or if gave up less than 5 years ago and any advice given by GP or any other relevant person

M130–24   (On any of these occasions) Did you have a discussion about giving up smoking, or were you just given something to take away and read?
IF BOTH CODE 1 FOR DISCUSSION

    (1) discussion
    (2) literature only

ask if: smokes now or if gave up less than 5 years ago and any advice given by GP or any other relevant person

M130–25   Did you find the advice helpful?

    (1) Yes
    (2) No

ask always:

M130–26a   There are some restrictions on cigarette advertising in the UK. As far as you are aware, is cigarette advertising allowed, not allowed or don't you know... On TV

    (1) cigarette advertising allowed
    (2) cigarette advertising not allowed
    (3) Don't know

ask always:

M130–26b   (As far as you are aware, is cigarette advertising allowed, not allowed or don't you know...) In newspapers and magazines

    (1) cigarette advertising allowed
    (2) cigarette advertising not allowed
    (3) Don't know

ask always:

M130–26c   (As far as you are aware, is cigarette advertising allowed, not allowed or don't you know...) At the cinema

    (1) cigarette advertising allowed
    (2) cigarette advertising not allowed
    (3) Don't know

ask always:

M130–26d   (As far as you are aware, is cigarette advertising allowed, not allowed or don't you know...) On radio

    (1) cigarette advertising allowed
    (2) cigarette advertising not allowed
    (3) Don't know

ask always:

M130–26e   (As far as you are aware, is cigarette advertising allowed, not allowed or don't you know...) Near hospitals

    (1) cigarette advertising allowed
    (2) cigarette advertising not allowed
    (3) Don't know

ask always:

M130–26f   (As far as you are aware, is cigarette advertising allowed, not allowed or don't you know...) Near schools

    (1) cigarette advertising allowed
    (2) ˉ cigarette advertising not allowed
    (3) Don't know

M130–26g   (As far as you are aware, is cigarette advertising allowed, not allowed or don't you know...)   In places where cigarettes are sold

    (1)   cigarette advertising allowed
    (2)   cigarette advertising not allowed
    (3)   Don't know

ask always:

m130–28a   Do you think the government should or should not allow tobacco advertising... on boardings and posters?

    (1)   should allow
    (2)   should not allow

ask always:

m130–28b   (Do you think the government should or should not allow tobacco advertising ...) in places where cigarettes are sold?

    (1)   should allow
    (2)   should not allow

ask always:

m130–28c   (Do you think the government should or should not allow tobacco advertising ...) in newspapers and magazines?

    (1)   should allow
    (2)   should not allow

ask always:

m130–28d   (Do you think the government should or should not allow tobacco advertising ...) of any kind at all?

    (1)   should allow
    (2)   should not allow

ask always:

m130–29a   How do you feel about tobacco companies being given publicity in return for sponsoring or supporting..   sports events?

    (1)   Approves strongly
    (2)   Approves
    (3)   Neither approves nor disapproves/doesn't mind
    (4)   Disapproves
    (5)   Disapproves strongly

ask always:

M130–29b   (How do you feel about tobacco companies being given publicity in return for sponsoring or supporting ...) events such as pop concerts?

    (1)   Approves strongly
    (2)   Approves
    (3)   Neither approves nor disapproves/doesn't mind
    (4)   Disapproves
    (5)   Disapproves strongly

ask always:

M130–29c   (How do you feel about tobacco companies being given publicity in return for sponsoring or supporting ...) opera or other arts events?

    (1)   Approves strongly
    (2)   Approves
    (3)   Neither approves nor disapproves/doesn't mind
    (4)   Disapproves
    (5)   Disapproves strongly

ask always:

M130–31   Do you think the government should increase the tax on cigarettes ... much more than the rate of inflation, just above the rate of inflation, only in line with inflation, or not at all?

RUNNING PROMPT
CODE ONE ONLY

    (1)   much more than the rate of inflation
    (2)   just above the rate of inflation
    (3)   only in line with inflation
    (4)   not at all

ask always:

M130–32A   Do you think that living with someone who smokes does, or does not, increase a child's risk of.. asthma

    (1)   increases risk
    (2)   does not increase risk

ask always:

M130–32b   (Do you think that living with someone who smokes does, or does not, increase a child's risk of..) glue ear?

    (1)   increases risk
    (2)   does not increase risk

M130–32c (Do you think that living with someone who smokes does, or does not, increase a child's risk of..) diabetes?

    (1) increases risk
    (2) does not increase risk

ask always:

M130–32d (Do you think that living with someone who smokes does, or does not, increase a child's risk of..) cot death?

    (1) increases risk
    (2) does not increase risk

ask always:

M130–32e (Do you think that living with someone who smokes does, or does not, increase a child's risk of..) chest infections?

    (1) increases risk
    (2) does not increase risk

ask always:

M130–32f (Do you think that living with someone who smokes does, or does not, increase a child's risk of..) other infections?

    (1) increases risk
    (2) does not increase risk

ask always:

m130–33a Do you think that breathing someone else's smoke increases the risk of a non-smoker getting.. asthma?

    (1) increases risk
    (2) does not increase risk

ask always:

m130–33b (Do you think that breathing someone else's smoke increases the risk of a non-smoker getting..) lung cancer?

    (1) increases risk
    (2) does not increase risk

ask always:

m130–33c (Do you think that breathing someone else's smoke increases the risk of a non-smoker getting..) diabetes?

    (1) increases risk
    (2) does not increase risk

ask always:

m130–33d (Do you think that breathing someone else's smoke increases the risk of a non-smoker getting..) heart disease?

    (1) increases risk
    (2) does not increase risk

ask always:

m130–33e (Do you think that breathing someone else's smoke increases the risk of a non-smoker getting..) bronchitis?

    (1) increases risk
    (2) does not increase risk

ask always:

m130–33f (Do you think that breathing someone else's smoke increases the risk of a non-smoker getting..) coughs and colds?

    (1) increases risk
    (2) does not increase risk

ask always:

m130–34a How far do you agree or disagree that there should be restrictions on smoking.. at work?

    (1) agrees strongly
    (2) agrees
    (3) Neither agrees nor disagrees/doesn't mind
    (4) Disagrees
    (5) Disagrees strongly

ask always:

m130–34b (How far do you agree or disagree that there should be restrictions on smoking..) in restaurants?

    (1) agrees strongly
    (2) agrees
    (3) Neither agrees nor disagrees/doesn't mind
    (4) Disagrees
    (5) Disagrees strongly

ask always:

m130–34c (How far do you agree or disagree that there should be restrictions on smoking..) in pubs?

    (1) agrees strongly
    (2) agrees
    (3) Neither agrees nor disagrees/doesn't mind
    (4) Disagrees
    (5) - Disagrees strongly

ask always:

m130–34d   (How far do you agree or disagree that there should be restrictions on smoking..) in public places such as banks and post offices?

    (1)   agrees strongly
    (2)   agrees
    (3)   Neither agrees nor disagrees/doesn't mind
    (4)   Disagrees
    (5)   Disagrees strongly

ask if: Only asked if currently working

M130–35   What sort of restrictions are there on smoking where you work?

    (1)   No smoking at all on the premises
    (2)   Smoking only allowed in designated smoking rooms
    (3)   No restrictions at all.
    (4)   Don't work in a building with other people